Anonymous

Pen and Pencil Pictures from the Poets

Anonymous

Pen and Pencil Pictures from the Poets

ISBN/EAN: 9783337778057

Printed in Europe, USA, Canada, Australia, Japan

Cover: Foto ©Thomas Meinert / pixelio.de

More available books at **www.hansebooks.com**

PEN AND PENCIL PICTURES

FROM

THE POETS.

WILLIAM P. NIMMO,
LONDON: 14 KING WILLIAM STREET, STRAND;
AND EDINBURGH.
1876.

CONTENTS.

	AUTHORS.	PAGE
THE SPIRIT OF POETRY,	*Longfellow*,	3
THE WEDDING PROCESSION OF ALDEN AND PRISCILLA,	*Longfellow*,	7
LOVE OF NATURE,	*N. P. Willis*,	8
AT NIGHT,	*Moore*,	11
HYMN OF THE CITY,	*W. C. Bryant*,	12
THE LIFE-BOAT,	*Moore*,	15
TO THE DAISY,	*Wordsworth*,	16
A COUNTRY WALK,	*Cowper*,	19
"EVENING STAR,"	*Wordsworth*,	23
TO THE CUCKOO,	*M. Bruce*,	24
SPRING,	*Thomson*,	27
TOWN AND COUNTRY LIFE,	*Cowper*,	28
EVANGELINE,	*Longfellow*,	31
THE VILLAGE,	*E. Elliot*,	32
AN ANCIENT PRUDE,	*Cowper*,	35
THE WRECK OF THE HESPERUS,	*Longfellow*,	39
SONNET,	*Wordsworth*,	45
A MOUNTAIN LANDSCAPE,	*Southey*,	46
SOLITUDE,	*Thomson*,	49
IL PENSEROSO,	*Milton*,	53
HAPPINESS OF A SHEPHERD'S LIFE,	*Shakespeare*,	54
SERENADE,	*Longfellow*,	57
PRAISE OF A COUNTRY LIFE,	*Sir H. Wotton*,	58

CONTENTS.

	AUTHORS.	PAGE
THE WANDERER,	Wordsworth, .	61
SABBATH MORNING, . .	J. Grahame,	64
THE VILLAGE ALE-HOUSE,	Goldsmith,	67
SUMMER, . .	Thomson,	71
CATTLE IN SUMMER, .	Thomson,	72
THE SOLDIER'S RETURN, .	Burns, .	75
SPRING, ...	T. Nash,	78
THE BAPTISM OF JESUS, .	Milton, .	81
THE CASTLE OF INDOLENCE,	Thomson,	85
A MADRIGAL,	Shakespeare, .	86
THE MESSIAH, .	Pope, .	89
EXCELSIOR, .	Longfellow, .	93
WINTER: A DIRGE, .	Burns, .	97
THE HAPPY HEART, . .	T. Dekker, .	98
APOSTROPHE TO NATURE,	A. Cunningham,	101
THE WOODMAN, . .	Cowper, .	105
THE LESSONS OF NATURE,	W. Drummond,	106
AFTON WATER, ...	Burns, . .	109
CHARACTER OF A HAPPY LIFE, .	Sir H. Wotton,	110
A CHURCHYARD SCENE,	J. Wilson,	113
RETURNING SPRING, .	Shelley, .	117
COUNSEL TO GIRLS, .	R. Herrick, .	118
ROBIN REDBREAST, .	Thomson,	121
THE TRUE BEAUTY, . . .	T. Carew,	122
MAN WAS MADE TO MOURN: A DIRGE, .	Burns, .	125
THE QUIET LIFE,	Pope, .	128
THE HERMIT, .	Goldsmith,	131
TWILIGHT, .	Wordsworth,	139
ECHOES, ...	Moore, .	140
A LESSON OF THANKFULNESS, .	Pope, . .	143
LOVE OF COUNTRY, .	Sir Walter Scott, .	147
THE WORLD'S WAY, .	Shakespeare, .	148
FREEDOM, . .	Cowper, .	151

ILLUSTRATIONS.

	DRAWN BY	ENGRAVED BY	PAGE
THE SPIRIT OF POETRY,	*Keeley Halswelle,*	*Pearson,*	2
THE WEDDING PROCESSION,	*Keeley Halswelle,*	*Pearson,*	6
AT NIGHT,	*Keeley Halswelle,*	*R. Paterson.*	10
THE LIFE-BOAT,	*Keeley Halswelle,*	*R. Paterson,*	14
A COUNTRY WALK,	*Hugh Cameron,*	*J. M. Corner,*	18
"EVENING STAR,"	*Keeley Halswelle,*	*J. M. Corner,*	22
SPRING,	*John M'Whirter,*	*J. M. Corner,*	26
EVANGELINE,	*Keeley Halswelle,*	*Pearson,*	30
AN ANCIENT PRUDE,	*Hugh Cameron,*	*J. M. Corner,*	34
THE WRECK OF THE HESPERUS,	*Keeley Halswelle,*	*J. Adam,*	38
SONNET,	*Keeley Halswelle,*	*J. M. Corner,*	44
SOLITUDE,	*John M'Whirter,*	*J. M. Corner,*	48
IL PENSEROSO,	*W. Smith,*	*F. Borders,*	52
A SERENADE,	*Keeley Halswelle,*	*T. Bolton,*	56
THE WANDERER,	*Keeley Halswelle,*	*R. Paterson,*	60
THE VILLAGE ALE-HOUSE,	*George Hay,*	*J. M. Corner,*	66
SUMMER,	*George Hay,*	*J. M. Corner,*	70
THE SOLDIER'S RETURN,	*J. Lawson,*	*R. Paterson.*	74

ILLUSTRATIONS.

	DRAWN BY	ENGRAVED BY	PAGE
THE BAPTISM OF JESUS,	W. Smith,	F. Borders,	80
THE CASTLE OF INDOLENCE,	John M'Whirter,	R. Paterson,	84
THE MESSIAH,	S. J. Groves,	F. Borders,	88
EXCELSIOR,	Keeley Halswelle,	T. Bolton,	92
WINTER: A DIRGE,	John M'Whirter,	R. Paterson.	96
APOSTROPHE TO NATURE,	John M'Whirter,	J. M. Corner,	100
THE WOODMAN,	Hugh Cameron,	J. M. Corner,	104
AFTON WATER,	George Hay,	R. Paterson,	108
A CHURCHYARD SCENE,	John M'Whirter,	J. Adam,	112
RETURNING SPRING,	John M'Whirter,	R. Paterson,	116
ROB'N REDBREAST,	John M'Whirter,	R. Paterson,	120
MAN WAS MADE TO MOURN,	S. Edmonston,	R. Paterson,	124
THE HERMIT,	George Hay,	R. Paterson,	130
TWILIGHT,	Keeley Halswelle,	T. Bolton,	138
A LESSON OF THANKFULNESS,	S. J. Groves,	F. Borders,	142
LOVE OF COUNTRY,	John M'Whirter,	R. Paterson,	146
FREEDOM,	Hugh Cameron,	R. Paterson,	150

PEN AND PENCIL PICTURES FROM THE POETS.

The Spirit of Poetry.

LONGFELLOW.

THERE is a quiet spirit in these woods,
    That dwells where'er the gentle south wind blows;
    Where, underneath the white thorn, in the glade,
    The wild flowers bloom, or, kissing the soft air,
    The leaves above their sunny palms outspread.
    With what a tender and impassioned voice
It fills the nice and delicate ear of thought,
When the fast-ushering star of morning comes
O'er-riding the gray hills with golden scarf;
Or when the cowled and dusky-sandall'd Eve,
In mourning weeds, from out the western gate,
Departs with silent pace! That spirit moves
In the green valley, where the silver brook,
From its full laver, pours the white cascade;
And, babbling low amid the tangled woods,
Slips down through moss-grown stones with endless laughter.
And frequent, on the everlasting hills,
Its feet go forth, when it doth wrap itself
In all the dark embroidery of the storm,
And shouts the stern, strong wind. And here, amid
The silent majesty of these deep woods,

Its presence shall uplift thy thoughts from earth,
As to the sunshine and the pure, bright air
Their tops the green trees lift. Hence gifted bards
Have ever loved the calm and quiet shades.
For them there was an eloquent voice in all
The sylvan pomp of woods, the golden sun,
The flowers, the leaves, the river on its way,
Blue skies, and silver clouds, and gentle winds,—
The swelling upland, where the sidelong sun
Aslant the wooded slope at evening goes,—
Groves, through whose broken roofs the sky looks in,
Mountain, and shattered cliff, and sunny vale,
The distant lake, fountains,—and mighty trees,
In many a lazy syllable, repeating
Their old poetic legends to the wind.
   And this is the sweet spirit that doth fill
The world; and in these wayward days of youth,
My busy fancy oft embodies it
As a bright image of the light and beauty
That dwell in nature,—of the heavenly forms
We worship in our dreams, and the soft hues
That stain the wild bird's wing, and flush the clouds
When the sun sets. Within her eye
The heaven of April, with its changing light,
And when it wears the blue of May, is hung,
And on her lip the rich, red rose. Her hair
Is like the summer tresses of the trees,
When twilight makes them brown, and on her cheek
Blushes the richness of an autumn sky,
With ever-shifting beauty. Then her breath,
It is so like the gentle air of Spring,
As, from the morning's dewy flowers, it comes
Full of their fragrance, that it is a joy
To have it round us,—and her silver voice
Is the rich music of a summer bird,
Heard in the still night, with its passionate cadence.

The Wedding Procession of Alden and Priscilla.

LONGFELLOW.

FROM a stall near at hand, amid exclamations of wonder,
Alden the thoughtful, the careful, so happy, so proud of Priscilla,
Brought out his snow-white steer, obeying the hand of its master,
Led by a cord that was tied to an iron ring in its nostrils,
Covered with crimson cloth, and a cushion placed for a saddle,
She should not walk, he said, through the dust and heat of the noonday;
Nay, she should ride like a queen, not plod along like a peasant.
Somewhat alarmed at first, but reassured by the others,
Placing her hand on the cushion, her foot in the hand of her husband,
Gaily, with joyous laugh, Priscilla mounted her palfrey.
"Nothing is wanting now," he said with a smile, "but the distaff;
Then you would be in truth my queen, my beautiful Bertha!"

Onward the bridal procession now moved to their new habitation,
Happy husband and wife, and friends conversing together.
Pleasantly murmured the brook, as they crossed the ford in the forest,
Pleased with the image that passed, like a dream of love through its bosom,
Tremulous, floating in air, o'er the depths of the azure abysses.
Down through the golden leaves the sun was pouring his splendours,
Gleaming on purple grapes, that, from branches above them suspended,
Mingled their odorous breath with the balm of the pine and the fir-tree,
Wild and sweet as the clusters that grew in the valley of Eshcol.
Like a picture it seemed of the primitive pastoral ages,
Fresh with the youth of the world, and recalling Rebecca and Isaac,
Old and yet ever new, and simple and beautiful always,
Love immortal and young in the endless succession of lovers.
So through the Plymouth woods passed onward the bridal procession.

Love of Nature.

N. P. WILLIS.

THERE is a gentler element, and man
   May breathe it with a calm unruffled soul,
   And drink its living waters till the heart
   Is pure.—And this is human happiness!
   Its secret and its evidence are writ
   In the broad book of nature. 'Tis to have
Attentive and believing faculties;
To go abroad rejoicing in the joy
Of beautiful and well-created things;
   To love the voice of waters, and the sheen
Of silver fountains leaping to the sea;
To thrill with the rich melody of birds
Living their life of music; to be glad
In the gay sunshine, reverent in the storm;
To see a beauty in the stirring leaf,
And find calm thoughts beneath the whispering tree;
To see, and hear, and breathe the evidence
Of God's deep wisdom in the natural world!

At Night.

MOORE.

AT night, when all is still around,
   How sweet to hear the distant sound
  Of footstep, coming soft and light!
  What pleasure in the anxious beat
  With which the bosom flies to meet
   That foot that comes so soft at night!

And then, at night, how sweet to say,
" 'Tis late, my love!" and chide delay,
  Though still the western clouds are bright;
Oh! happy, too, the silent press,
The eloquence of mute caress,
  With those we love exchanged at night!

Hymn of the City.

W. C. Bryant.

Not in the solitude
Alone may man commune with Heaven, or see
    Only in savage wood
And sunny vale the present Deity;
    Or only hear His voice
Where the winds whisper and the waves rejoice.

    Even here do I behold
Thy steps, Almighty!—here, amidst the crowd
    Through the great city rolled,
With everlasting murmur, deep and loud—
    Choking the ways that wind
'Mongst the proud piles, the work of human kind.

    Thy golden sunshine comes
From the round heaven, and on their dwellings lies,
    And lights their inner homes;
For them thou fill'st with air the unbounded skies,
    And givest them the stores
Of ocean, and the harvests of its shores.

    Thy Spirit is around,
Quickening the restless mass that sweeps along;
    And this eternal sound—
Voices and footfalls of the numberless throng—
    Like the resounding sea,
Or like the rainy tempest, speaks of Thee.

    And when the hours of rest
Come, like a calm upon the mid-sea brine,
    Hushing its billowy breast,
The quiet of that moment too is Thine;
    It breathes of Him who keeps
The vast and helpless city while it sleeps.

The Life-Boat.

Moore.

'TIS sweet to behold, when the billows are sleeping,
    Some gay-coloured bark moving gracefully by ;
No damp on her deck but the even-tide's weeping,
    No breath in her sails but the summer-wind's sigh.

Yet who would not turn with a fonder emotion,
    To gaze on the life-boat, though rugged and worn,
Which often hath wafted o'er hills of the ocean,
    The lost light of hope to the seaman forlorn !

Oh ! grant that of those who in life's sunny slumber
    Around us like summer-barks idly have played,
When storms are abroad we may find in the number
    One friend, like the life-boat, to fly to our aid.

To the Daisy.

Wordsworth.

BRIGHT flower, whose home is everywhere!
A pilgrim bold in Nature's care,
And all the long year through the heir
    Of joy or sorrow,
Methinks that there abides in thee
Some concord with humanity,
Given to no other flower I see
    The forest thorough!

Is it that man is soon deprest?
A thoughtless thing! who, once unblest,
Does little on his memory rest
    Or on his reason,
And thou wouldst teach him how to find
A shelter under every wind,
A hope for times that are unkind
    And every season?

Thou wanderest the wide world about,
Unchecked by pride or scrupulous doubt,
With friends to greet thee, or without,
    Yet pleased and willing;
Meek, yielding to occasion's call,
And all things suffering from all,
Thy function apostolical
    In peace fulfilling.

c

A Country Walk.

COWPER.

HERE unmolested, through whatever sign
The sun proceeds, I wander: neither mist
Nor freezing sky, nor sultry, checking me,
Nor stranger intermeddling with my joy.
Even in the spring and playtime of the year,
That calls the unwonted villager abroad
With all her little ones, a sportive train,
To gather kingcups in the yellow mead,
And prink their hair with daisies, or to pick
A cheap but wholesome salad from the brook,
These shades are all my own. The timorous hare,
Grown so familiar with her frequent guest,
Scarce shuns me; and the stockdove, unalarmed,
Sits cooing in the pine-tree, nor suspends
His long love-ditty for my near approach.
Drawn from his refuge in some lonely elm
That age or injury has hallowed deep,
Where, on his bed of wool and matted leaves,
He has outslept the winter, ventures forth
To frisk a while, and bask in the warm sun,
The squirrel, flippant, pert, and full of play.
He sees me, and at once, swift as a bird,
Ascends the neighbouring beech; there whisks his brush,
And perks his ears, and stamps and scolds aloud,
With all the prettiness of feigned alarm,
And anger insignificantly fierce.
 The heart is hard in nature, and unfit
For human fellowship, as being void

Of sympathy, and therefore dead alike
To love and friendship both, that is not pleased
With sight of animals enjoying life,
Nor feels their happiness augment his own.
The bounding fawn that darts across the glade
When none pursues, through mere delight of heart,
And spirits buoyant with excess of glee;
The horse, as wanton and almost as fleet,
That skims the spacious meadow at full speed,
Then stops and snorts, and throwing high his heels,
Starts to the voluntary race again;
The very kine that gambol at high noon,
The total herd receiving first from one
That leads the dance a summons to be gay,
Though wild their strange vagaries, and uncouth
Their efforts, yet resolved with one consent
To give such act and utterance as they may
To ecstasy too big to be suppressed;
These, and a thousand images of bliss,
With which kind nature graces every scene
Where cruel man defeats not her design,
Impart to the benevolent, who wish
All that are capable of pleasure pleased,
A far superior happiness to theirs,
The comfort of a reasonable joy.

"Evening Star."

WORDSWORTH.

THEIR cottage on a plot of rising ground
    Stood single, with large prospect, north and south,
    High into Easedale, up to Dunmal-Raise,
    And westward to the village near the lake;
    And from this constant light, so regular
    And so far seen, the house itself, by all
Who dwelt within the limits of the vale,
Both old and young, was named the "Evening Star."

To the Cuckoo.

M. Bruce

Hail, beauteous stranger of the grove!
   Thou messenger of Spring!
Now heaven repairs thy rural seat,
   And woods thy welcome sing.

What time the daisy decks the green,
   Thy certain voice we hear;
Hast thou a star to guide thy path,
   Or mark the rolling year?

Delightful visitant! with thee
   I hail the time of flowers,
And hear the sound of music sweet
   From birds among the bowers.

The schoolboy, wandering through the wood
   To pull the primrose gay,
Starts, the new voice of Spring to hear,
   And imitates thy lay.

What time the pea puts on the bloom,
   Thou fliest thy vocal vale,
An annual guest in other lands,
   Another Spring to hail.

Oh, could I fly, I'd fly with thee!
   We'd make, with joyful wing,
Our annual visits o'er the globe,
   Companions of the Spring.

D

Spring.

Thomson.

NOW from the town,
Buried in smoke, and sleep, and noisome damps,
Oft let me wander o'er the dewy fields,
Where freshness breathes, and dash the trembling drops
From the bent bush, as through the verdant maze
Of sweetbrier-hedges I pursue my walk ;
Or taste the smell of dairy ; or ascend
Some eminence, Augusta, in thy plains,
And see the country, far diffused around,
One boundless blush, one white-empurpled shower
Of mingled blossoms : where the raptured eye
Hurries from joy to joy ; and, hid beneath
The fair profusion, yellow Autumn spies.

Town and Country Life.

COWPER.

GOD made the country, and man made the town.
What wonder, then, that health and virtue—gifts
That can alone make sweet the bitter draught
That life holds out to all—should most abound
And least be threatened, in the fields and groves!
Possess ye therefore, ye who, borne about
In chariots and sedans, know no fatigue
But that of idleness, and taste no scenes,
But such as art contrives, possess ye still
Your element; there only can ye shine;
There only minds like yours can do no harm.
Our groves were planted to console at noon
The pensive wanderer in their shades. At eve,
The moonbeam, sliding softly in between
The sleeping leaves, is all the light they wish;
Birds warbling, all the music. We can spare
The splendour of your lamps; they but eclipse
Our softer satellite. Your songs confound
Our more harmonious notes: the thrush departs
Scared, and the offended nightingale is mute.
There is a public mischief in your mirth;
It plagues your country. Folly such as yours,
Graced with a sword, and worthier of a fan,
Has made—what enemies could ne'er have done—
Our arch of empire, steadfast but for you,
A mutilated structure, soon to fall.

Evangeline.

Longfellow.

EVANGELINE brought the draught-board out of its corner.
   Soon was the game begun. In friendly contention the
      old men
   Laughed at each lucky hit or unsuccessful manœuvre,
   Laughed when a man was crowned, or a breach was
      made in the king-row.
   Meanwhile, apart, in the twilight gloom of a window's embra-
      sure,
   Sat the lovers, and whispered together, beholding the moon
      rise
Over the pallid sea and the silvery mist of the meadows.
Silently, one by one, in the infinite meadows of heaven,
Blossomed the lovely stars, the forget-me-nots of the angels.
Thus passed the evening away.

The Village.

E. Elliot.

SWEET village! where my early days were passed,
Though parted long, we meet, we meet at last!
Like friends, imbrowned by many a sun and wind,
Much changed in mien, but more in heart and mind,
Fair, after many years, thy fields appear,
With joy beheld, but not without a tear.
I met thy little river miles before
I saw again my natal cottage door;
Unchanged as truth, the river welcomed home
The wanderer of the sea's heart-breaking foam;
But the changed cottage, like a time-tried friend,
Smote on my heart-strings, at my journey's end.
For now no lilies bloom the door beside!
The very house-leek on the roof hath died!
The windowed gable's ivy bower is gone,
The rose departed from the porch of stone:
The pink, the violet, have fled away,
The polyanthus and auricula!
And round my home, once bright with flowers, I found
Not one square yard, one foot of garden ground.
Path of the quiet fields! that oft of yore
Called me at morn on Shenstone's page to pore;
Oh! poor man's pathway! where, "at evening's close,"
He stopped to pluck the woodbine and the rose,
Shaking the dew-drop from the wild-brier bowers,
That stooped beneath their load of summer flowers,
Then eyed the west, still bright with fading flame,
As whistling homeward by the wood he came;
Sweet, dewy, sunny, flowery footpath, thou
Art gone for ever, like the poor man's cow!

An Ancient Prude.

COWPER.

YON ancient prude, whose withered features show
She might be young some forty years ago,
Her elbows pinioned close upon her hips,
Her head erect, her fan upon her lips,
Her eyebrows arched, her eyes both gone astray
To watch yon amorous couple in their play,
With bony and unkerchiefed neck defies
The rude inclemency of wintry skies,
And sails with lappet head and mincing airs
Duly at clink of bell to morning prayers.
To thrift and parsimony much inclined,
She yet allows herself that boy behind;
The shivering urchin, bending as he goes,
With slipshod heels, and dewdrop at his nose,
His predecessor's coat advanced to wear,
Which future pages yet are doomed to share,
Carries her Bible tucked beneath his arm,
And hides his hands to keep his fingers warm.
She, half an angel in her own account,
Doubts not hereafter with the saints to mount,
Though not a grace appears on strictest search,
But that she fasts, and *item*, goes to church.
Conscious of age, she recollects her youth,
And tells, not always with an eye to truth,
Who spanned her waist, and who, where'er he came,
Scrawled upon glass Miss Bridget's lovely name,
Who stole her slipper, filled it with tokay,
And drank the little bumper every day.

Of temper as envenomed as an asp,
Censorious, and her every word a wasp,
In faithful memory she records the crimes,
Or real, or fictitious, of the times ;
Laughs at the reputations she has torn,
And holds them dangling at arm's length in scorn.
  Such are the fruits of sanctimonious pride,
Of malice fed while flesh is mortified :
Take, madam, the reward of all your prayers,
Where hermits and where Brahmins meet with theirs ;
Your portion is with them ; nay, never frown,
But, if you please, some fathoms lower down.

The Wreck of the Hesperus.

Longfellow.

'T was the schooner Hesperus,
    That sailed the wintry sea;
And the skipper had taken his little daughter,
    To bear him company.

Blue were her eyes as the fairy-flax,
    Her cheeks like the dawn of day,
And her bosom white as the hawthorn buds,
    That ope in the month of May.

The skipper he stood beside the helm,
    His pipe was in his mouth,
And he watched how the veering flaw did blow
    The smoke now west, now south.

Then up and spake an old sailor,
    Had sailed the Spanish Main,
"I pray thee, put into yonder port,
    For I fear a hurricane.

"Last night the moon had a golden ring,
    And to-night no moon we see!"
The skipper he blew a whiff from his pipe,
    And a scornful laugh laughed he.

Colder and louder blew the wind,
　　A gale from the north-east;
The snow fell hissing in the brine,
　　And the billows frothed like yeast.

Down came the storm, and smote amain
　　The vessel in its strength;
She shuddered and paused, like a frighted steed,
　　Then leaped a cable's length.

"Come hither! come hither! my little daughter,
　　And do not tremble so;
For I can weather the roughest gale,
　　That ever wind did blow."

He wrapped her warm in his seaman's coat
　　Against the stinging blast;
He cut a rope from a broken spar,
　　And bound her to the mast.

"O father! I hear the church-bells ring,
　　Oh, say, what may it be?"
"'Tis a fog-bell on a rock-bound coast!"
　　And he steered for the open sea.

"O father! I hear the sound of guns,
　　Oh, say, what may it be?"
"Some ship in distress that cannot live
　　In such an angry sea!"

"O father, I see a gleaming light,
　　Oh, say, what may it be?"
But the father answered never a word,
　　A frozen corpse was he.

Lashed to the helm, all stiff and stark,
    With his face turned to the skies,
The lantern gleamed through the gleaming snow
    On his fixed and glassy eyes.

Then the maiden clasped her hands and prayed
    That savèd she might be;
And she thought of Christ, who stilled the wave
    On the Lake of Galilee.

And fast through the midnight dark and drear,
    Through the whistling sleet and snow,
Like a sheeted ghost, the vessel swept
    Towards the reef of Norman's Woe.

And ever the fitful gusts between
    A sound came from the land;
It was the sound of the trampling surf,
    On the rocks and the hard sea-sand.

The breakers were right beneath her bows,
    She drifted a dreary wreck,
And a whooping billow swept the crew
    Like icicles from her deck.

She struck where the white and fleecy waves
    Looked soft as carded wool,
But the cruel rocks, they gored her side,
    Like the horns of an angry bull.

Her rattling shrouds, all sheathed in ice,
    With the masts went by the board;
Like a vessel of glass, she stove and sank,
    Ho! ho! the breakers roared!

At daybreak, on the bleak sea-beach,
    A fisherman stood aghast,
To see the form of a maiden fair,
    Lashed close to a drifting mast.

The salt sea was frozen on her breast,
    The salt tears in her eyes;
And he saw her hair, like the brown sea-weed,
    On the billows fall and rise.

Such was the wreck of the Hesperus,
    In the midnight and the snow!
Christ save us all from a death like this,
    On the reef of Norman's Woe!

Sonnet.

Wordsworth.

With ships the sea was sprinkled far and nigh,
Like stars in heaven, and joyously it showed;
Some lying fast at anchor in the road,
Some veering up and down, one knew not why.
A goodly vessel did I then espy
Come like a giant from a haven broad;
And lustily along the bay she strode,
"Her tackling rich, and of apparel high."
This ship was naught to me, nor I to her,
Yet I pursued her with a lover's look;
This ship to all the rest did I prefer:
When will she turn, and whither? She will brook
No tarrying; where she comes the winds must stir:
On went she,—and due north her journey took.

A Mountain Landscape.

Southey.

A LITTLE way
    He turned aside, by natural impulses
    Moved, to behold Cadwallon's lonely hut,
    That lonely dwelling stood among the hills,
    By a gray mountain's stream; just elevate
Above the winter torrents did it stand,
Upon a craggy bank; an orchard slope
Arose behind, and joyous was the scene,
    In early summer, when those antic trees
Shone with their blushing blossoms, and the flax
Twinkled beneath the breeze its liveliest green.
But, save the flax-field and that orchard slope,
All else was desolate, and now all wore
One sober hue; the narrow vale, which wound
Among the hills, was gray with rocks, that peered
Above its shallow soil; the mountain side
Was with loose stones bestrewn, which oftentimes
Sliding beneath the foot of straggling goat,
Clattered adown the steep; or huger crags,
Which, when the coming frost should loosen them,
Would thunder down. . . . .
              Adown the vale,
Broken by stones, and o'er a stony bed,
Roared the loud mountain stream.

Solitude.

Thomson.

SEE the fading many-coloured woods,
    Shade deepening over shade, the country round
    Imbrown; a crowded umbrage, dusk, and dun,
    Of every hue, from wan declining green
    To sooty dark. These now the lonesome muse,
    Low-whispering, lead into their leaf-strown walks;
    And give the season in its latest view.
Meantime, light shadowing all, a sober calm
Fleeces unbounded ether; whose least wave
Stands tremulous, uncertain where to turn
The gentle current: while, illumined wide,
The dewy-skirted clouds imbibe the sun,
And through their lucid veil his softened force
Shed o'er the peaceful world. Then is the time
For those whom wisdom and whom nature charm
To steal themselves from the degenerate crowd,
And soar above this little scene of things;
To tread low-thoughted vice beneath their feet,
To soothe the throbbing passions into peace,
And woo lone quiet in her silent walks,
    Thus solitary, and in pensive guise,
Oft let me wander o'er the russet mead,
And through the saddened grove, where scarce is heard
One dying strain to cheer the woodman's toil.
Haply some widowed songster pours his plaint,
Far, in faint warblings, through the tawny copse;
While congregated thrushes, linnets, larks,
And each wild throat, whose artless strains so late

Swelled all the music of the swarming shades,
Robbed of their tuneful souls, now shivering sit
On the dead tree, a dull despondent flock!
With not a brightness waving o'er their plumes,
And nought save chattering discord in their note.
Oh, let not, aimed from some inhuman eye,
The gun the music of the coming year
Destroy; and harmless, unsuspecting harm,
Lay the weak tribes, a miserable prey,
In mingled murder, fluttering on the ground!

Il Penseroso.

Milton.

Hence, vain deluding joys,
    The brood of Folly, without father bred!
    How little you bested,
        Or fill the fixed mind with all your toys!
    Dwell in some idle brain,
    And fancies fond with gaudy shapes possess,
    As thick and numberless
    As the gay motes that people the sunbeams,
    Or likest hovering dreams,
The fickle pensioners of Morpheus' train.
But, hail! thou goddess sage and holy,
Hail! divinest Melancholy!
Whose saintly visage is too bright
To hit the sense of human sight,
And, therefore, to our weaker view,
O'erlaid with black, staid Wisdom's hue;
Black, but such as in esteem
Prince Memnon's sister might beseem,
Or that starred Ethiop queen that strove
To set her beauty's praise above
The sea-nymphs, and their powers offended:
Yet thou art higher far descended;
Thee, bright-haired Vesta, long of yore,
To solitary Saturn bore;
His daughter she; in Saturn's reign
Such mixture was not held a stain:
Oft in glimmering bowers and glades
He met her, and in secret shades
Of woody Ida's inmost grove,
Whilst yet there was no fear of Jove.

Happiness of a Shepherd's Life.

SHAKESPEARE.

METHINKS it were a happy life
To be no better than a homely swain;
To sit upon a hill, as I do now,
To carve out dials quaintly, point by point,
Thereby to see the minutes how they run:
How many make the hour full complete,
How many hours bring about the day,
How many days will finish up the year,
How many years a mortal man may live.
When this is known, then to divide the times:
So many hours must I tend my flock;
So many hours must I take rest;
So many hours must I contemplate;
So many hours must I sport myself;
So many days my ewes have been with young;
So many weeks ere the poor fools will yean;
So many years ere I shall shear the fleece;
So minutes, hours, days, weeks, months, and years,
Passed over to the end they were created,
Would bring white hairs unto a quiet grave.
Ah! what a life were this! how sweet—how lovely!

. . . . .

And to conclude,—the shepherd's homely curds,
His cold thin drink out of his leather bottle,
His wonted sleep under a fresh tree's shade,
All which secure and sweetly he enjoys,
Is far beyond a prince's delicates,
His viands sparkling in a golden cup,
His body couched on a curious bed,
When care, mistrust, and treason wait on him.

Serenade.

LONGFELLOW.

STARS of the summer night!
    Far in yon azure deeps,
Hide, hide your golden light!
    She sleeps!
My lady sleeps!
    Sleeps!

Moon of the summer night!
    Far down yon western steeps
Sink, sink in silver light!
    She sleeps!
My lady sleeps!
    Sleeps!

Wind of the summer night!
    Where yonder woodbine creeps,
Fold, fold thy pinions light!
    She sleeps!
My lady sleeps!
    Sleeps!

Dreams of the summer night!
    Tell her, her lover keeps
Watch! while in slumbers light
    She sleeps!
My lady sleeps!
    Sleeps!

Praise of a Country Life.

Sir H. Wotton.

MISTAKEN mortals! did you know
Where joy, heart's-ease, and comforts, grow,
    You'd scorn proud towers,
    And seek them in these bowers;
Where winds sometimes our woods perhaps may shake,
But blustering care could never tempest make,
    Nor murmurs e'er come nigh us,
    Save of fountains that glide by us.

Here's no fantastic masque or dance,
But of our kids that frisk and prance;
    Nor wars are seen,
    Unless upon the green
Two harmless lambs are butting one another—
Which done, both bleating run each to his mother;
    And wounds are never found,
    Save what the ploughshare gives the ground.

Go! let the diving negro seek
For gems hid in some forlorn creek;
    We all perils scorn,
    Save what the dewy morn
Congeals upon each little spire of grass,
Which careless shepherds beat down as they pass;
    And gold ne'er here appears,
    Save what the yellow harvest bears

The Wanderer

WORDSWORTH.

THERE is often found
  In mournful thoughts, and always might be found,
  A power to virtue friendly: were 't not so,
  I am a dreamer among men, indeed
  An idle dreamer! 'Tis a common tale,
  An ordinary sorrow of man's life,
A tale of silent suffering, hardly clothed
In bodily form. But, without further bidding,
I will proceed. " While thus it fared with them,
To whom this cottage, till those hapless years,
Had been a blessèd home, it was my chance
To travel in a country far remote;
And glad I was, when, halting by yon gate
That leads from the green lane, once more I saw
These lofty elm-trees. Long I did not rest:
With many pleasant thoughts I cheered my way
O'er the flat common. Having reached the door,
I knocked; and when I entered with the hope
Of usual greeting, Margaret looked at me
A little while; then turned her head away
Speechless; and, sitting down upon a chair,
Wept bitterly. I wist not what to do,
Or how to speak to her. Poor wretch! at last
She rose from off her seat, and then,—oh, sir!
I cannot *tell* how she pronounced my name.
With fervent love, and with a face of grief

Unutterably helpless, and a look
That seemed to cling upon me, she inquired
If I had seen her husband. As she spake,
A strange surprise and fear came to my heart,
Nor had I power to answer ere she told
That he had disappeared—not two months gone,
He left his house; two wretched days had passed,
And on the third, as wistfully she raised
Her head from off her pillow, to look forth,
Like one in trouble, for returning light,
Within her chamber casement she espied
A folded paper, lying as if placed
To meet her waking eyes. This tremblingly
She opened—found no writing, but therein
Pieces of money carefully enclosed.
Silver and gold—' I shuddered at the sight,'
Said Margaret, ' for I knew it was his hand
Which placed it there ; and, ere that day was ended,
That long and anxious day! I learned from one
Sent hither by my husband to impart
The heavy news, that he had joined a troop
Of soldiers going to a distant land.
He left me thus—he could not gather heart
To take a farewell of me ; for he feared
That I should follow with my babes, and sink
Beneath the misery of that wandering life.'

"This tale did Margaret tell with many tears;
And, when she ended, I had little power
To give her comfort, and was glad to take
Such words of hope from her own mouth as served
To cheer us both; but long we had not talked,
Ere we built up a pile of better thoughts,
And with a brighter eye she looked around
As if she had been shedding tears of joy.
We parted. 'Twas the time of early spring;

I left her busy with her garden tools;
And well remember, o'er that fence she looked,
And, while I paced along the foot-way path,
Called out, and sent a blessing after me,
With tender cheerfulness; and with a voice
That seemed the very sound of happy thoughts.

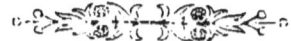

Sabbath Morning.

JAMES GRAHAME.

How still the morning of the hallowed day!
Mute is the voice of rural labour, hushed
The ploughboy's whistle and the milkmaid's song.
The scythe lies glittering in the dewy wreath
Of tedded grass, mingled with fading flowers,
That yester-morn bloomed waving in the breeze:
Sounds the most faint attract the ear,—the hum
Of early bee, the trickling of the dew,
The distant bleating midway up the hill.
Calmness sits throned on yon unmoving cloud.
To him who wanders o'er the upland leas,
The blackbird's note comes mellower from the dale;
And sweeter from the sky the gladsome lark
Warbles his heaven-tuned song; the lulling brook
Murmurs more gently down the deepworn glen;
While from yon lowly roof, whose curling smoke
O'ermounts the mist, is heard, at intervals,
The voice of psalms,—the simple song of praise.
With dove-like wings, Peace o'er yon village broods;
The dizzying mill-wheel rests; the anvil's din
Hath ceased: all, all around is quietness.
Less fearful on this day, the limping hare
Stops, and looks back, and stops, and looks on man,
Her deadliest foe; the toil-worn horse, set free,
Unheedful of the pasture, roams at large;
And, as his stiff unwieldy bulk he rolls,
His iron-armed hoofs gleam in the morning ray.

I

The Village Ale-House.

GOLDSMITH.

NEAR yonder thorn, that lifts its head on high,
Where once the sign-post caught the passing eye,
Low lies that house, where nut-brown draughts inspired,
Where gray-beard mirth, and smiling toil retired,
Where village statesmen talked with looks profound,
And news much older than their ale went round.
Imagination fondly stoops to trace
The parlour splendours of that festive place;
The white-washed wall, the nicely-sanded floor,
The varnished clock that clicked behind the door;
The chest contrived a double debt to pay,
A bed by night, a chest of drawers by day;
The pictures placed for ornament and use,
The Twelve Good Rules, the royal game of Goose;
The hearth, except when winter chilled the day,
With aspen boughs, and flowers and fennel gay;
While broken tea-cups, wisely kept for show,
Ranged o'er the chimney, glistened in a row.

Vain transitory splendours! could not all
Reprieve the tottering mansion from its fall?
Obscure it sinks, nor shall it more impart
An hour's importance to the poor man's heart;
Thither no more the peasant shall repair,
To sweet oblivion of his daily care;
No more the farmer's news, the barber's tale,
No more the woodman's ballad shall prevail;

No more the smith his dusky brow shall clear,
Relax his ponderous strength, and lean to hear;
The host himself no longer shall be found
Careful to see the mantling bliss go round;
Nor the coy maid, half willing to be pressed,
Shall kiss the cup to pass it to the rest.

Summer.

Thomson.

NOW swarms the village o'er the joyful mead:
The rustic youth, brown with meridian toil,
Healthful and strong; full as the summer rose
Blown by prevailing suns, the ruddy maid,
Half-naked, swelling on the sight, and all
Her kindled graces burning o'er her cheek.
Even stooping age is here; and infant hands
Trail the long rake, or, with the fragrant load
O'ercharged, amid the kind oppression roll.
Wide flies the tedded grain; all in a row
Advancing broad, or wheeling round the field,
They spread their breathing harvest to the sun,
That throws refreshful round a rural smell;
Or, as they rake the green-appearing ground,
And drive the dusky wave along the mead,
The russet haycock rises thick behind,
In order gay: while heard from dale to dale,
Waking the breeze, resounds the blended voice
Of happy labour, love, and social glee.

Cattle in Summer.

Thomson.

AROUND th' adjoining brook, that purls along
    The vocal grove now fretting o'er a rock,
    Now scarcely moving through a reedy pool,
    Now starting to a sudden stream, and now
    Gently diffused into a limpid plain
A various group the herds and flocks compose.
Rural confusion! on the grassy bank
Some ruminating lie; while others stand
Half in the flood, and often bending sip
The circling surface. In the middle droops
The strong laborious ox, of honest front,
Which incomposed he shakes; and from his sides
The troublous insects lashes with his tail,
Returning still. Amid his subjects safe,
Slumbers the monarch swain; his careless arm
Thrown round his head, on downy moss sustained;
Here laid his scrip, with wholesome viands filled;
There, listening every noise, his watchful dog.
    Light fly his slumbers, if perchance a flight
Of angry gadflies fasten on the herd;
That startling scatters from the shallow brook,
In search of lavish stream. Tossing the foam,
They scorn the keeper's voice, and scour the plain,
Through all the bright severity of noon;
While, from their labouring breasts, a hollow moan
Proceeding, runs low-bellowing round the hills.

κ

The Soldier's Return.

BURNS.

WHEN wild war's deadly blast was blawn,
   And gentle peace returning,
Wi' mony a sweet babe fatherless,
   And mony a widow mourning;
I left the lines and tented field,
   Where lang I'd been a lodger,
My humble knapsack a' my wealth,
   A poor and honest sodger.

A leal light heart was in my breast,
   My hand unstained wi' plunder,
And for fair Scotia, hame again,
   I cheery on did wander.
I thought upon the banks o' Coil,
   I thought upon my Nancy,
I thought upon the witching smile
   That caught my youthful fancy.

At length I reached the bonny glen
   Where early life I sported;
I passed the mill, and trysting thorn,
   Where Nancy aft I courted:
Wha spied I but my ain dear maid,
   Down by her mother's dwelling!
And turned me round to hide the flood
   That in my een was swelling.

Wi' altered voice, quoth I, "Sweet lass,
    Sweet as yon hawthorn's blossom,
Oh! happy, happy may he be,
    That's dearest to thy bosom!
My purse is light, I've far to gang,
    And fain wad be thy lodger;
I've served my king and country lang—
    Take pity on a sodger."

Sae wistfully she gazed on me,
    And lovelier was than ever;
Quo' she, "A sodger ance I lo'ed,
    Forget him shall I never:
Our humble cot, and hamely fare,
    Ye freely shall partake it,
That gallant badge—the dear cockade—
    Ye're welcome for the sake o't."

She gazed—she reddened like a rose—
    Syne pale like ony lily;
She sank within my arms, and cried,
    "Art thou my ain dear Willie?"
"By Him who made yon sun and sky,
    By whom true love's regarded,
I am the man; and thus may still
    True lovers be rewarded!

"The wars are o'er, and I'm come hame,
    And find thee still true-hearted;
Though poor in gear, we're rich in love,
    And mair, we'se ne'er be parted."
Quo' she, "My grandsire left me gowd,
    A mailen plenished fairly;
And come, my faithful sodger lad,
    'Thou'rt welcome to it dearly!"

For gold the merchant ploughs the main,
    The farmer ploughs the manor;
But glory is the sodger's prize,
    The sodger's wealth is honour:
The brave poor sodger ne'er despise,
    Nor count him as a stranger;
Remember, he's his country's stay
    In day and hour of danger.

Spring.

J. Nash.

SPRING! the sweet Spring! is the year's pleasant king:
  Then blooms each thing, then maids dance in a ring;
  Cold doth not sting, the pretty birds do sing,
    Cuckoo, jug-jug, pu-we, to-witta-woo!

The palm and may make country houses gay,
  Lambs frisk and play, the shepherds pipe all day;
  And we hear aye birds tune this merry lay,
    Cuckoo, jug-jug, pu-we, to-witta-woo!

The fields breathe sweet, the daisies kiss our feet,
Young lovers meet, old wives a-sunning sit;
In every street these tunes our ears do greet,
   Cuckoo, jug-jug, pu-we, to-witta-woo!
    Spring! the sweet Spring!

The Baptism of Jesus.

MILTON.

High are Thy thoughts,
O Son; but nourish them, and let them soar
To what height sacred virtue and true worth
Can raise them, though above example high:
By matchless deeds express Thy matchless Sire,
For know, Thou art no Son of mortal man;
Though men esteem Thee low of parentage,
Thy Father is the eternal King, who rules
All heaven and earth, angels and sons of men;
A messenger from God foretold Thy birth
Conceived in me a virgin; He foretold
Thou shouldst be great, and sit on David's throne,
And of Thy kingdom there should be no end.
At Thy nativity, a glorious quire
Of angels, in the fields of Bethlehem, sung
To shepherds, watching at their folds by night,
And told them the Messiah now was born,
Where they might see Him, and to Thee they came.
Directed to the manger where Thou lay'st,
For in the inn was left no better room:
A star, not seen before, in heaven appearing,
Guided the wise men thither from the east,
To honour Thee with incense, myrrh, and gold;
By whose bright course led on they found the place,
Affirming it Thy star, new-graven in heaven,
By which they knew the King of Israel born.
Just Simeon and prophetic Anna, warned
By vision, found Thee in the temple, and spake,
Before the altar and the vested priest,
Like things of Thee to all that present stood.

"This having heard, straight I again revolved
The law and prophets, searching what was writ
Concerning the Messiah, to our scribes
Known partly, and soon found of whom they spake
I am; this chiefly, that my way must lie
Through many a hard assay, even to the death,
Ere I the promised kingdom can attain,
Or work redemption for mankind, whose sins'
Full weight must be transferred upon my head.
Yet, neither thus disheartened, nor dismayed,
The time prefixed I waited; when, behold
The Baptist, (of whose birth I oft had heard,
Not knew by sight,) now come, who was to come,
Before Messiah, and His way prepare!
I, as all others, to his baptism came,
Which I believed was from above; but he
Straight knew me, and with loudest voice proclaimed
Me Him, (for it was shown him so from heaven,)
Me Him, whose harbinger he was; and first
Refused on me his baptism to confer,
As much his greater, and was hardly won:
But, as I rose out of the laving stream,
Heaven opened her eternal doors, from whence
The Spirit descended on me like a dove;
And last, the sum of all, my Father's voice,
Audibly heard from heaven, pronounced me His,
Me His beloved Son, in whom alone
He was well pleased; by which I knew the time
Now full, that I no more should live obscure;
But openly begin, as best becomes
The authority which I derived from heaven.
And now by some strong motion I am led
Into this wilderness, to what intent
I learn not yet: perhaps I need not know,
For what concerns my knowledge God reveals."

The Castle of Indolence.

Thomson.

IN lowly dale, fast by a river's side,
    With woody hill o'er hill encompassed round,
    A most enchanting wizard did abide,
    Than whom a fiend more fell is nowhere found.
It was, I ween, a lovely spot of ground ;
    And there a season atween June and May,
    Half prankt with spring, with summer half imbrowned
    A listless climate made, where, sooth to say,
No living wight could work, ne cared even for play.

    Was nought around but images of rest ;
    Sleep-soothing groves, and quiet lawns between ;
    And flowery beds that slumbrous influence kest,
    From poppies breathed ; and beds of pleasant green,
    Where never yet was creeping creature seen.
    Meantime, unnumbered glittering streamlets played,
    And hurlèd everywhere their waters sheen ;
    That, as they bickered through the sunny glade,
Though restless still themselves, a lulling murmur made.

A Madrigal.

Shakespeare.

CRABBED Age and Youth
Cannot live together:
Youth is full of pleasance,
Age is full of care;
Youth like summer morn,
Age like winter weather,
Youth like summer brave,
Age like winter bare:
Youth is full of sport,
Age's breath is short,
Youth is nimble, Age is lame:
Youth is hot and bold,
Age is weak and cold,
Youth is wild, and Age is tame:—
Age, I do abhor thee,
Youth, I do adore thee;
Oh! my Love, my Love is young!
Age, I do defy thee—
O sweet shepherd, hie thee,
For methinks thou stay'st too long.

The Messiah.

Pope.

THUS shall mankind His guardian care engage,
The promised Father of the future age.
No more shall nation against nation rise,
Nor ardent warriors meet with hateful eyes,
Nor fields with gleaming steel be covered o'er,
The brazen trumpets kindle rage no more;
But useless lances into scythes shall bend,
And the broad falchion in a ploughshare end.
Then palaces shall rise; the joyful son
Shall finish what his short-lived sire begun;
Their vines a shadow to their race shall yield,
And the same hand that sowed shall reap the field.
The swain in barren deserts with surprise
See lilies spring, and sudden verdure rise;
And start, amidst the thirsty wilds, to hear
New falls of water murmuring in his ear.
On rifted rocks, the dragon's late abodes,
The green reed trembles, and the bulrush nods.
Waste sandy valleys, once perplexed with thorn,
The spiry fir and shapely box adorn;
To leafless shrubs the flowering palms succeed,
And odorous myrtle to the noisome weed.
The lambs with wolves shall graze the verdant mead,
And boys in flowery bands the tiger lead;
The steer and lion at one crib shall meet,
And harmless serpents lick the pilgrim's feet.
The smiling infant in his hand shall take
The crested basilisk and speckled snake,

Pleased the green lustre of the scales survey,
And with their forky tongue shall innocently play.
Rise, crowned with light, imperial Salem, rise !
Exalt thy towery head, and lift thy eyes !
See, a long race thy spacious courts adorn ;
See future sons, and daughters yet unborn,
In crowding ranks on every side arise,
Demanding life, impatient for the skies !
See barbarous nations at thy gates attend,
Walk in thy light, and in thy temple bend ;
See thy bright altars thronged with prostrate kings,
And heaped with products of Sabean springs,
For thee Idume's spicy forests blow,
And seeds of gold in Ophir's mountains glow.
See heaven its sparkling portals wide display,
And break upon thee in a flood of day.
No more the rising sun shall gild the morn,
Nor evening Cynthia fill her silver horn ;
But lost, dissolved in thy superior rays,
One tide of glory, one unclouded blaze
O'erflows thy courts ; the Light himself shall shine
Revealed, and God's eternal day be thine !
The seas shall waste, the skies in smoke decay,
Rocks fall to dust, and mountains melt away ;
But fixed His word, His saving power remains :
Thy realm for ever lasts, thy own Messiah reigns.

Excelsior.

LONGFELLOW.

THE shades of night were falling fast,
As through an Alpine village passed
A youth, who bore, 'mid snow and ice,
A banner with the strange device,
    Excelsior!

His brow was sad; his eye beneath,
Flashed like a falchion from its sheath,
And like a silver clarion rung
The accents of that unknown tongue,
    Excelsior!

In happy homes he saw the light
Of household fires gleam warm and bright;
Above, the spectral glaciers shone,
And from his lips escaped a groan,
    Excelsior!

"Try not the Pass!" the old man said;
"Dark lowers the tempest overhead,
The roaring torrent is deep and wide!"
And loud that clarion voice replied,
    Excelsior!

"Oh, stay," the maiden said, "and rest
Thy weary head upon this breast!"
A tear stood in his bright blue eye,
But still he answered, with a sigh,
    Excelsior!

" Beware the pine-tree's withered branch!
Beware the awful avalanche!"
This was the peasant's last Good-night;
A voice replied, far up the height,
    Excelsior!

At break of day, as heavenward
The pious monks of St Bernard
Uttered the oft-repeated prayer,
A voice cried through the startled air,
    Excelsior!

A traveller, by the faithful hound,
Half-buried in the snow was found,
Still grasping in his hand of ice
That banner with the strange device,
    Excelsior!

There in the twilight cold and gray,
Lifeless, but beautiful, he lay,
And from the sky, serene and far,
A voice fell, like a falling star,
    Excelsior!

Winter: a Dirge.

Burns.

THE wintry west extends his blast,
    And hail and rain does blaw;
Or, the stormy north sends driving forth
    The blinding sleet and snaw:
While tumbling brown, the burn comes down,
    And roars frae bank to brae;
And bird and beast in covert rest,
    And pass the heartless day.

" The sweeping blast, the sky o'ercast,"
    The joyless winter-day,
Let others fear, to me more dear
    Than all the pride of May:
The tempest's howl, it soothes my soul,
    My griefs it seems to join;
The leafless trees my fancy please,
    Their fate resembles mine!

Thou Power Supreme, whose mighty scheme
    These woes of mine fulfil,
Here, firm, I rest, they must be best,
    Because they are Thy will!
Then all I want (oh, do Thou grant
    This one request of mine!)
Since to enjoy Thou dost deny,
    Assist me to resign.

The Happy Heart.

T. Dekker.

ART thou poor, yet hast thou golden slumbers?
        O sweet content!
Art thou rich, yet is thy mind perplexèd?
        O punishment!
Dost thou laugh to see how fools are vexèd
To add to golden numbers, golden numbers!
O sweet content! O sweet, O sweet content!
    Work apace, apace, apace, apace;
    Honest labour bears a lovely face;
Then hey nonny nonny, hey nonny nonny!

Canst drink the waters of the crispèd spring?
        O sweet content!
Swimm'st thou in wealth, yet sink'st in thine own tears?
        O punishment!
Then he that patiently wants burden bears,
No burden bears, but is a king, a king!
O sweet content! O sweet, O sweet content!
    Work apace, apace, apace, apace;
    Honest labour bears a lovely face;
Then hey nonny nonny, hey nonny nonny!

Apostrophe to Nature.

A. CUNNINGHAM

NATURE! holy, meek, and mild,
Thou dweller on the mountain wild;
Thou haunter of the lonesome wood;
Thou wanderer by the secret flood;
Thou lover of the daisied sod,
Where Spring's white foot hath lately trod;
Finder of flowers fresh-sprung and new,
Where sunshine comes to seek the dew;
Twiner of bowers for lovers meet;
Smoother of sods for poets' feet;
Thrice-sainted matron! in whose face,
Who looks in love will light on grace;
Far-worshipped goddess! one who gives
Her love to him who wisely lives;—
Oh! take my hand and place me on
The daisied footstool of thy throne;
And pass before my darkened sight
Thy hand which lets in charmèd light;
And touch my soul, and let me see
The ways of God, fair dame, in thee.

Or lead me forth o'er dales and meads,
Even as her child the mother leads;
Where corn, yet milk in its green ears,
The dew upon its shot-blade bears;
Where blooming clover grows, and where
She licks her scented foot, the hare;
Where twin-nuts cluster thick, and springs

The thistle with ten thousand stings;
Untrodden flowers and unpruned trees,
Gladdened with songs of birds and bees;
The ring where last the fairies danced—
The place where dank Will latest glanced—
The tower round which the magic shell
Of minstrel threw its lasting spell—
The stream that steals its way along,
To glory consecrate by song:
And while we saunter, let thy speech
God's glory and His goodness preach.

Or, when the sun sinks, and the bright
Round moon sheds down her lustrous light;
When larks leave song, and men leave toiling;
And hearths burn clear, and maids are smiling;
When hoary hinds, with rustic saws,
Lay down to youth thy golden laws;
And beauty is her wet cheek laying
To her sweet child, and silent praying;
With thee in hallowed mood I'll go,
Through scenes of gladness or of woe:
Thy looks inspired, thy chastened speech,
Me more than man hath taught shall teach;
And much that's gross, and more that's vain,
As chaff from corn, shall leave my strain.

I feel thy presence and thy power,
As feels the rain yon parchèd flower;
It lifts its head, spreads forth its bloom,
Smiles to the sky, and sheds perfume.
A child of woe, sprung from the clod,
Through thee seeks to ascend to God.

The Woodman.

Cowper.

Forth goes the woodman, leaving unconcerned
The cheerful haunts of man, to wield the axe
And drive the wedge in yonder forest drear,
From morn to eve his solitary task.
Shaggy, and lean, and shrewd, with pointed ears
And tail cropped short, half lurcher and half cur,
His dog attends him. Close behind his heel
Now creeps he slow; and now with many a frisk
Wide scampering, snatches up the drifted snow
With ivory teeth, or ploughs it with his snout;
Then shakes his powdered coat, and barks for joy.
Heedless of all his pranks, the sturdy churl
Moves right toward the mark; nor stops for aught,
But now and then with pressure of his thumb
To adjust the fragrant charge of a short tube
That fumes beneath his nose: the trailing cloud
Streams far behind him, scenting all the air.

The Lessons of Nature:

W. Drummond.

If this fair volume which we World do name
If we the sheets and leaves could turn with care,
Of Him who it corrects, and did it frame,
We clear might read the art and wisdom rare:

Find out His power which wildest powers doth tame,
His providence extending everywhere,
His justice which proud rebels doth not spare,
In every page, no period of the same.

But silly we, like foolish children, rest
Well pleased with coloured vellum, leaves of gold,
Fair dangling ribbands, leaving what is best,
On the great writer's sense ne'er taking hold;

Or if by chance we stay our minds on aught,
It is some picture on the margin wrought.

Afton Water.

Burns.

Flow gently, sweet Afton, among thy green braes,
Flow gently, I'll sing thee a song in thy praise;
My Mary's asleep by thy murmuring stream—
Flow gently, sweet Afton, disturb not her dream.

Thou stock-dove, whose echo resounds through the glen,
Ye wild whistling blackbirds in yon thorny den,
Thou green-crested lapwing, thy screaming forbear--
I charge you disturb not my slumbering fair.

How lofty, sweet Afton, thy neighbouring hills,
Far marked with the courses of clear winding rills;
There daily I wander, as noon rises high,
My flocks and my Mary's sweet cot in my eye.

How pleasant thy banks and green valleys below,
Where wild in the woodlands the primroses blow;
There, oft as mild evening weeps over the lea,
The sweet-scented birk shades my Mary and me.

Thy crystal stream, Afton, how lovely it glides,
And winds by the cot where my Mary resides;
How wanton thy waters her snowy feet lave,
As gathering sweet flowerets she stems thy clear wave.

Flow gently, sweet Afton, among thy green braes,
Flow gently, sweet river, the theme of my lays;
My Mary's asleep by thy murmuring stream—
Flow gently, sweet Afton, disturb not her dream!

Character of a Happy Life.

Sir H. Wotton.

How happy is he born and taught
That serveth not another's will;
Whose armour is his honest thought,
And simple truth his utmost skill!

Whose passions not his masters are,
Whose soul is still prepared for death,
Not tied unto the world with care
Of public fame, or private breath;

Who envies none that chance doth raise
Or vice; who never understood
How deepest wounds are given by praise;
Nor rules of state, but rules of good:

Who hath his life from rumours freed,
Whose conscience is his strong retreat;
Whose state can neither flatterers feed,
Nor ruin make accusers great;

Who God doth late and early pray
More of His grace than gifts to lend;
And entertains the harmless day
With a well-chosen book or friend.

This man is freed from servile bands
Of hope to rise, or fear to fall;
Lord of himself, though not of lands;
And having nothing, yet hath all.

A Churchyard Scene.

J. WILSON.

HOW sweet and solemn, all alone,
    With reverend steps, from stone to stone,
    In a small village churchyard lying,
    O'er intervening flowers to move!
And as we read the names unknown
Of young and old to judgment gone,
And hear in the calm air above
    Time onwards softly flying,
    To meditate, in Christian love,
    Upon the dead and dying!
Across the silence seem to go
With dream-like motion, wavering, slow,
And shrouded in their folds of snow,
The friends we loved, long, long ago!
Gliding across the sad retreat,
How beautiful their phantom feet!
What tenderness is in their eyes,
Turned where the poor survivor lies
'Mid monitory sanctities!
What years of vanished joy are fanned
From one uplifting of that hand,
In its white stillness! when the shade
Doth glimmeringly in sunshine fade
From our embrace, how dim appears
This world's life through a mist of tears!
Vain hopes! blind sorrows! needless fears!
Such is the scene around me now:
A little churchyard on the brow

Of a green pastoral hill;
Its sylvan village sleeps below,
And faintly there is heard the flow
Of Woodburn's summer rill;
A place where all things mournful meet,
And yet the sweetest of the sweet,
The stillest of the still!
With what a pensive beauty fall
Across the mossy mouldering wall
That rose-tree's clustered arches! see
The robin-redbreast warily,
Bright, through the blossoms, leaves his nest;
Sweet ingrate! through the winter blest
At the firesides of men—but shy—
Through all the sunny summer hours,
He hides himself among the flowers,
In his own wild festivity.
What lulling sound, and shadow cool,
Hangs half the darken'd churchyard o'er,
From thy green depths so beautiful,
Thou gorgeous sycamore!
Oft hath the holy wine and bread
Been blest beneath thy murmuring tent,
Where many a bright and hoary head
Bowed at that awful sacrament.
Now all beneath the turf are laid,
On which they sat, and sang, and prayed.
Above that consecrated tree
Ascends the tapering spire, that seems
To lift the soul up silently
To heaven, with all its dreams;
While in the belfry, deep and low,
From his heaved bosom's purple gleams
The dove's continuous murmurs flow,
A dirge-like song, half bliss, half woe,
The voice so lonely seems!

Returning Spring.

SHELLEY.

OH, woe is me! Winter is come and gone,
   But grief returns with the revolving year;
   The airs and streams renew their joyous tone;
   The ants, the bees, the swallows, reappear;
   Fresh leaves and flowers deck the dead season's bier.
   The loving birds now pair in every brake,
   And build their mossy homes in field and brere;
   And the green lizard and the golden snake,
Like unimprison'd flames, out of their trance awake.

Through wood and stream, and field and hill and ocean,
A quickening life from the earth's heart has burst,
As it has ever done, with change and motion,
From the great morning of the world! when first
God dawned on chaos; in its stream immersed,
The lamps of heaven flash with a softer light;
All baser things pant with life's sacred thirst;
Diffuse themselves; and spend in love's delight
The beauty and the joy of their renewèd might.

Counsel to Girls.

R. Herrick.

Gather ye rosebuds while ye may,
    Old Time is still a-flying:
And this same flower that smiles to-day,
    To-morrow will be dying.

The glorious Lamp of Heaven, the Sun,
    The higher he's a-getting,
The sooner will his race be run,
    The nearer he's to setting.

That age is best which is the first,
    When youth and blood are warmer;
But being spent, the worse, and worst
    Times, still succeed the former.

Then be not coy, but use your time;
    And while ye may, go marry:
For having lost but once your prime,
    You may for ever tarry.

Robin Redbreast.

THOMSON.

THE cherished fields
Put on their winter robe of purest white.
'Tis brightness all; save where the new snow melts
Along the mazy current. Low the woods
Bow their hoar head; and, ere the languid sun
Faint from the west emits his evening ray,
Earth's universal face, deep-hid and chill,
Is one wild dazzling waste, that buries wide
The works of man. Drooping, the labourer-ox
Stands covered o'er with snow, and then demands
The fruit of all his toil. The fowls of heaven,
Tamed by the cruel season, crowd around
The winnowing store, and claim the little boon
Which Providence assigns them. One alone,
The redbreast, sacred to the household gods,
Wisely regardful of the embroiling sky,
In joyless fields and thorny thickets leaves
His shivering mates, and pays to trusted man
His annual visit. Half-afraid, he first
Against the window beats; then, brisk, alights
On the warm hearth; then, hopping o'er the floor,
Eyes all the smiling family askance,
And pecks, and starts, and wonders where he is—
Till, more familiar grown, the table-crumbs
Attract his slender feet.

The True Beauty.

T. CAREW.

He that loves a rosy cheek
  Or a coral lip admires,
Or from star-like eyes doth seek,
  Fuel to maintain his fires;
As old Time makes these decay,
So his flames must waste away.

But a smooth and steadfast mind,
  Gentle thoughts, and calm desires,
Hearts with equal love combined,
  Kindle never-dying fires:
Where these are not, I despise
Lovely cheeks or lips or eyes.

Man was made to Mourn: a Dirge.

Burns.

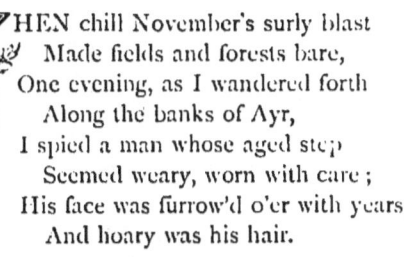

WHEN chill November's surly blast
    Made fields and forests bare,
One evening, as I wandered forth
    Along the banks of Ayr,
I spied a man whose aged step
    Seemed weary, worn with care;
His face was furrow'd o'er with years,
    And hoary was his hair.

"Young stranger, whither wanderest thou?"
    Began the reverend sage;
"Does thirst of wealth thy step constrain,
    Or youthful pleasures rage?
Or haply, prest with cares and woes,
    Too soon thou hast began
To wander forth with me to mourn
    The miseries of man.

"The sun that overhangs yon moors,
    Outspreading far and wide,
Where hundreds labour to support
    A haughty lordling's pride:
I've seen yon weary winter sun
    Twice forty times return,
And every time has added proofs
    That man was made to mourn.

"O man! while in thy early years,
  How prodigal of time!
Misspending all thy precious hours,
  Thy glorious youthful prime!
Alternate follies take the sway;
  Licentious passions burn;
Which tenfold force gives nature's law,
  That man was made to mourn.

"Look not alone on youthful prime,
  Or manhood's active might;
Man then is useful to his kind,
  Supported is his right:
But see him on the edge of life,
  With cares and sorrows worn;
Then age and want—oh! ill-matched pair!—
  Show man was made to mourn.

"A few seem favourites of fate,
  In pleasure's lap carest;
Yet think not all the rich and great
  Are likewise truly blest.
But, oh! what crowds in every land
  Are wretched and forlorn!
Through weary life this lesson learn—
  That man was made to mourn.

"Many and sharp the numerous ills
  Inwoven with our frame!
More pointed still we make ourselves—
  Regret, remorse, and shame!
And man, whose heaven-erected face
  The smiles of love adorn,
Man's inhumanity to man
  Makes countless thousands mourn!

"See yonder poor, o'erlaboured wight,
 So abject, mean, and vile,
Who begs a brother of the earth
 To give him leave to toil;
And see his lordly fellow-worm
 The poor petition spurn,
Unmindful, though a weeping wife
 And helpless offspring mourn.

"If I'm designed yon lordling's slave—
 By nature's law designed—
Why was an independent wish
 E'er planted in my mind?
If not, why am I subject to
 His cruelty or scorn?
Or why has man the will and power
 To make his fellow mourn?

"Yet let not this too much, my son,
 Disturb thy youthful breast;
This partial view of humankind
 Is surely not the last!
The poor, oppressèd, honest man,
 Had never, sure, been born,
Had there not been some recompense
 To comfort those that mourn.

"O Death! the poor man's dearest friend—
 The kindest and the best!
Welcome the hour my agèd limbs
 Are laid with thee at rest!
The great, the wealthy, fear thy blow,
 From pomp and pleasure torn;
But, oh! a blest relief to those
 That weary-laden mourn!"

The Quiet Life.

Pope.

Happy the man, whose wish and care
A few paternal acres bound,
Content to breathe his native air
    In his own ground.

Whose herds with milk, whose fields with bread,
Whose flocks supply him with attire;
Whose trees in summer yield him shade,
    In winter, fire.

Blest, who can unconcernedly find
Hours, days, and years, slide soft away
In health of body, peace of mind,
    Quiet by day.

Sound sleep by night; study and ease
Together mixed; sweet recreation,
And innocence, which most does please
    With meditation.

Thus let me live, unseen, unknown;
Thus unlamented let me die;
Steal from the world, and not a stone
    Tell where I lie.

The Hermit.

Goldsmith.

"Turn, gentle Hermit of the dale,
  And guide my lonely way,
To where yon taper cheers the vale
  With hospitable ray.

"For here forlorn and lost I tread,
  With fainting steps and slow;
Where wilds, immeasurably spread,
  Seem lengthening as I go."

"Forbear, my son," the Hermit cries,
  "To tempt the dangerous gloom:
For yonder faithless phantom flies
  To lure thee to thy doom.

"Here to the houseless child of want
  My door is open still;
And though my portion is but scant,
  I give it with good-will.

"Then turn to-night, and freely share
  Whate'er my cell bestows;
My rushy couch and frugal fare,
  My blessing and repose.

"No flocks that range the valley free,
 To slaughter I condemn;
Taught by that Power that pities me,
 I learn to pity them:

"But from the mountain's grassy side
 A guiltless feast I bring;
A scrip with herbs and fruits supplied,
 And water from the spring.

"Then pilgrim, turn; thy cares forego;
 All earth-born cares are wrong;
'Man wants but little here below,
 Nor wants that little long.'"

Soft as the dew from heaven descends,
 His gentle accents fell;
The modest stranger lowly bends,
 And follows to the cell.

Far in a wilderness obscure
 The lonely mansion lay,
A refuge to the neighbouring poor,
 And strangers led astray.

No stores beneath its humble thatch
 Required a master's care;
The wicket, opening with a latch,
 Received the harmless pair.

And now, when busy crowds retire
 To take their evening rest,
The Hermit trimmed his little fire,
 And cheered his pensive guest.

And spread his vegetable store,
    And gaily pressed, and smiled;
And, skilled in legendary lore,
    The lingering hours beguiled.

Around in sympathetic mirth
    Its tricks the kitten tries,
The cricket chirrups in the hearth,
    The crackling faggot flies.

But nothing could a charm impart
    To soothe the stranger's woe;
For grief was heavy at his heart,
    And tears began to flow.

His rising cares the Hermit spied,
    With answering care oppressed:
"And whence, unhappy youth," he cried,
    "The sorrows of thy breast?

"From better habitations spurned,
    Reluctant dost thou rove?
Or grieve for friendship unreturned,
    Or unregarded love?

"Alas! the joys that fortune brings
    Are trifling, and decay;
And those who prize the trifling things,
    More trifling still than they.

"And what is friendship but a name;
    A charm that lulls to sleep;
A shade that follows wealth or fame,
    But leaves the wretch to weep?

"And love is still an emptier sound,
    The modern fair one's jest :
On earth unseen, or only found
    To warm the turtle's nest.

"For shame, fond youth! thy sorrows hush,
    And spurn the sex," he said ;
But while he spoke, a rising blush
    His love-lorn guest betrayed.

Surprised he sees new beauties rise,
    Swift mantling to the view ;
Like colours o'er the morning skies,
    As bright, as transient too.

The bashful look, the rising breast,
    Alternate spread alarms :
The lovely stranger stands confessed,
    A maid in all her charms.

"And, ah! forgive a stranger rude,
    A wretch forlorn," she cried ;
"Whose feet unhallowed thus intrude
    Where heaven and you reside.

"But let a maid thy pity share,
    Whom love has taught to stray :
Who seeks for rest, but finds despair
    Companion of her way.

"My father lived beside the Tyne,
    A wealthy lord was he ;
And all his wealth was marked as mine ;
    He had but only me.

"To win me from his tender arms,
　　Unnumbered suitors came;
Who praised me for imputed charms,
　　And felt, or feigned a flame.

"Each hour a mercenary crowd
　　With richest proffers strove;
Amongst the rest young Edwin bowed,
　　But never talked of love.

"In humble, simplest habit clad,
　　No wealth nor power had he;
Wisdom and worth were all he had,
　　But these were all to me.

"And when beside me in the dale
　　He carolled lays of love,
His breath lent fragrance to the gale,
　　And music to the grove.

"The blossom opening to the day,
　　The dews of heaven refined,
Could naught of purity display
　　To emulate his mind.

"The dew, the blossom on the tree,
　　With charms inconstant shine;
Their charms were his, but woe to me!
　　Their constancy was mine.

"For still I tried each fickle art,
　　Importunate and vain;
And while his passion touched my heart,
　　I triumphed in his pain:

"Till quite dejected with my scorn,
   He left me to my pride;
And sought a solitude forlorn,
   In secret, where he died.

"But mine the sorrow, mine the fault,
   And well my life shall pay:
I'll seek the solitude he sought,
   And stretch me where he lay.

"And there, forlorn, despairing, hid,
   I'll lay me down and die;
'Twas so for me that Edwin did;
   And so for him will I."

"Forbid it, Heaven!" the Hermit cried,
   And clasped her to his breast:
The wondering fair one turned to chide,—
   'Twas Edwin's self that pressed.

"Turn, Angelina, ever dear,
   My charmer, turn to see
Thy own, thy long-lost Edwin here,
   Restored to love and thee.

"Thus let me hold thee to my heart,
   And every care resign:
And shall we never, never part,
   My life, my all that's mine?

"No, never from this hour to part,
   We'll live and love so true;
The sigh that rends thy constant heart
   Shall break thy Edwin's too."

s

Twilight.

Wordsworth.

Hail, Twilight, sovereign of one peaceful hour!
   Not dull art thou as undiscerning Night!
   But studious only to remove from sight
   Day's mutable distinctions. Ancient power!
   Thus did the waters gleam, the mountains lower
To the rude Briton, when in wolf-skin vest
Here roving wild, he laid him down to rest
On the bare rock, or through a leafy bower
Looked ere his eyes were closed. By him was seen
The self-same vision which we now behold,
At thy meek bidding, shadowy power, brought forth;
These mighty barriers, and the gulf between;
The floods—the stars; a spectacle as old
As the beginning of the heavens and earth!

Echoes.

Moore.

HOW sweet the answer Echo makes
    To Music at night
When, roused by lute or horn, she wakes,
And far away o'er lawns and lakes
    Goes answering light!

Yet Love hath echoes truer far
    And far more sweet
Than e'er, beneath the moonlight's star,
Of horn or lute or soft guitar
    The songs repeat.

'Tis when the sigh,—in youth sincere,
    And only then,
The sigh that's breathed for one to hear—
Is by that one, that only dear,
    Breathed back again.

A Lesson of Thankfulness.

Pope.

HEAVEN from all creatures hides the book of Fate,
All but the page prescribed, their present state;
From brutes what men, from men what spirits know:
Or who could suffer being here below?
The lamb thy riot dooms to bleed to-day,
Had he thy reason, would he skip and play?
Pleased to the last he crops the flowery food,
And licks the hand just raised to shed his blood.
Oh, blindness to the future! kindly given,
That each may fill the circle marked by Heaven.

. . . . . .

Hope humbly, then; with trembling pinions soar;
Wait the great teacher, Death; and God adore.
What future bliss, He gives not thee to know,
But gives that hope to be thy blessing now.
Hope springs eternal in the human breast:
Man never *is*, but always *to be* blest:
The soul, uneasy and confined from home,
Rests and expatiates in a life to come.
 Lo, the poor Indian, whose untutored mind
Sees God in clouds, and hears Him in the wind;
His soul proud science never taught to stray
Far as the solar walk or milky way;
Yet simple nature to his hope has given,
Behind the cloud-topped hill, an humbler heaven;
Some safer world in depth of woods embraced,
Some happier island in the watery waste,

Where slaves once more their native land behold,
No fiends torment, nor Christians thirst for gold.
To *be*, contents his natural desire,
He asks no angel's wing, no seraph's fire;
But thinks, admitted to that equal sky,
His faithful dog shall bear him company.

   Go, wiser thou, and in thy scale of sense
Weigh thy opinion against Providence;
Call imperfection what thou fanciest such;
Say, Here He gives too little, there too much:
Destroy all creatures for thy sport or gust,
Yet cry, if man's unhappy, God's unjust;
If man alone engross not Heaven's high care,
Alone made perfect here, immortal there;
Snatch from His hand the balance and the rod,
Re-judge His justice, be the God of God.

1.

Love of Country.

Sir Walter Scott.

BREATHES there the man, with soul so dead,
  Who never to himself hath said,
    This is my own, my native land!
  Whose heart hath ne'er within him burned,
  As home his footsteps he hath turned
    From wandering on a foreign strand!—
If such there breathe, go, mark him well;
For him no minstrel raptures swell;
High though his titles, proud his name,
Boundless his wealth as wish can claim;
Despite those titles, power, and pelf,
The wretch concentred all in self,
Living, shall forfeit fair renown,
And, doubly dying, shall go down
To the vile dust, from whence he sprung,
Unwept, unhonoured, and unsung.

O Caledonia! stern and wild,
Meet nurse for a poetic child!
Land of brown heath and shaggy wood,
Land of the mountain and the flood,
Land of my sires! what mortal hand
Can e'er untie the filial band
That knits me to thy rugged strand!

The World's Way.

Shakespeare.

TIRED with all these, for restful death I cry—
As, to behold desert a beggar born,
And needy nothing trimmed in jollity,
And purest faith unhappily forsworn,

And gilded honour shamefully misplaced,
And maiden virtue rudely strumpeted,
And right perfection wrongfully disgraced,
And strength by limping sway disabled,

And art made tongue-tied by authority,
And folly, doctor-like, controlling skill,
And simple truth miscalled simplicity,
And captive Good attending captain Ill :—

Tired with all these, from these would I be gone,
Save that, to die, I leave my Love alone.

Freedom.

Cowper.

ASK not the boy, who, when the breeze of morn
First shakes the glittering drops from every thorn,
Unfolds his flock, then under bank or bush
Sits linking cherry-stones, or platting rush,
How fair is freedom?—he was always free:
To carve his rustic name upon a tree,
To snare the mole, or with ill-fashioned hook
To draw the incautious minnow from the brook,
Are life's prime pleasures in his simple view,
His flock the chief concern he ever knew;
She shines but little in his heedless eyes,
The good we never miss we rarely prize.
But ask the noble drudge in state affairs,
Escaped from office and its constant cares,
What charms he sees in Freedom's smile expressed,
In freedom lost so long, now repossessed;
The tongue whose strains were cogent as commands,
Revered at home, and felt in foreign lands,
Shall own itself a stammerer in that cause,
Or plead its silence as its best applause.
He knows indeed that whether dressed or rude,
Wild without art, or artfully subdued,
Nature in every form inspires delight,
But never marked her with so just a sight.
Her hedge-row shrubs, a variegated store,
With woodbine and wild roses mantled o'er,
Green balks and furrowed lands, the stream that spreads
Its cooling vapour o'er the dewy meads.

Downs that almost escape the inquiring eye,
That melt and fade into the distant sky,
Beauties he lately slighted as he passed,
Seem all created since he travelled last.
Master of all the enjoyments he designed,
No rough annoyance rankling in his mind,
What early philosophic hours he keeps,
How regular his meals, how sound he sleeps;
Not sounder he that on the mainmast head,
While morning kindles with a windy red,
Begins a long look-out for distant land,
Nor quits till evening watch his giddy stand,
Then swift descending with a seaman's haste,
Slips to his hammock, and forgets the blast.

www.ingramcontent.com/pod-product-compliance
Lightning Source LLC
Chambersburg PA
CBHW030310170426
43202CB00009B/946